Table of Contents

CHAPTER 1

What Is a Star?

After the Sun sets, little dots of light appear in the sky. Before long, you can see thousands. Some people think they look like diamonds. Others see bright crosses. What do you think these are? **Stars**? What do you think a star is?

sky full of stars

A star is a huge ball of very hot and fiery **gas** in space. The gas burns and makes a lot of light and heat, just like a gigantic fire.

hot and fiery star

When we look into the night sky, we see huge stars that are millions of miles wide. They are so far away that they look tiny from here on Earth.

SMART WORDS

gas: a substance like air that does not have a hard surface

star: a huge ball of very hot and glowing gases

The Solar System

Our Sun is also a star. It is the center of our solar system. A solar system is like a neighborhood in space. But the solar system neighborhood is made up of the Sun, planets, moons, and other objects.

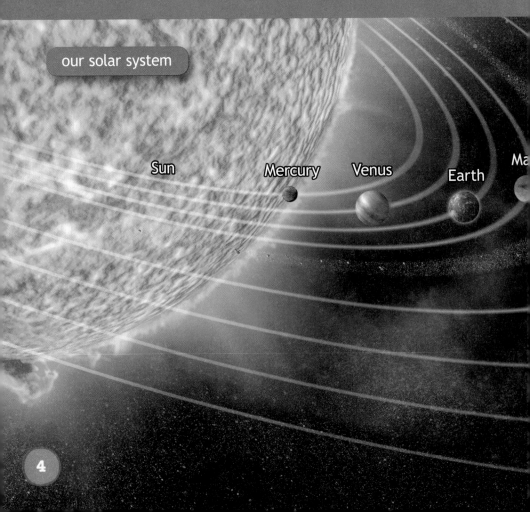

our solar system

Sun   Mercury   Venus   Earth   Ma[...]

Other stars we see may be suns in other solar systems. Our Sun looks very big because it is much closer to us than other stars.

We are so close to the Sun that we can feel its heat and enjoy its light. The Sun is the only object in our solar system that makes light and heat.

Jupiter

Saturn

Uranus

Neptune

The Milky Way

Our solar system may seem big. But it is just a very small part of our **galaxy**. A galaxy is a huge group of stars. Many of these stars have their own solar systems. We can see only a few of the many stars in our galaxy!

the Milky Way

Our galaxy is called the **Milky Way**. Why do you think it is called the Milky Way?

Long ago people looked up at the sky on very clear nights and thought the stars looked like milk had been spilled across the sky.

the Milky Way

SMART WORDS

galaxy: a large group of stars

Milky Way: our galaxy, which includes our solar system and many others

The Universe

How many stars do you think there are? Scientists think there are billions and billions of stars. That's more than the grains of sand on all the beaches on Earth!

billions of stars

The Milky Way has lots of stars. But it is just one of billions of galaxies in our **universe**.

another galaxy in our universe

The universe is made up of everything in space — our solar system, the Milky Way, and all the other galaxies, too.

SMART WORD

universe: all of space and everything in it, including all solar systems and galaxies

my place in the universe

me

Earth

solar system

Milky Way (galaxy)

universe

9

USE YOUR SMART WORDS

Use your Smart Words to complete the crosswor

galaxy gas Milky Way
star universe

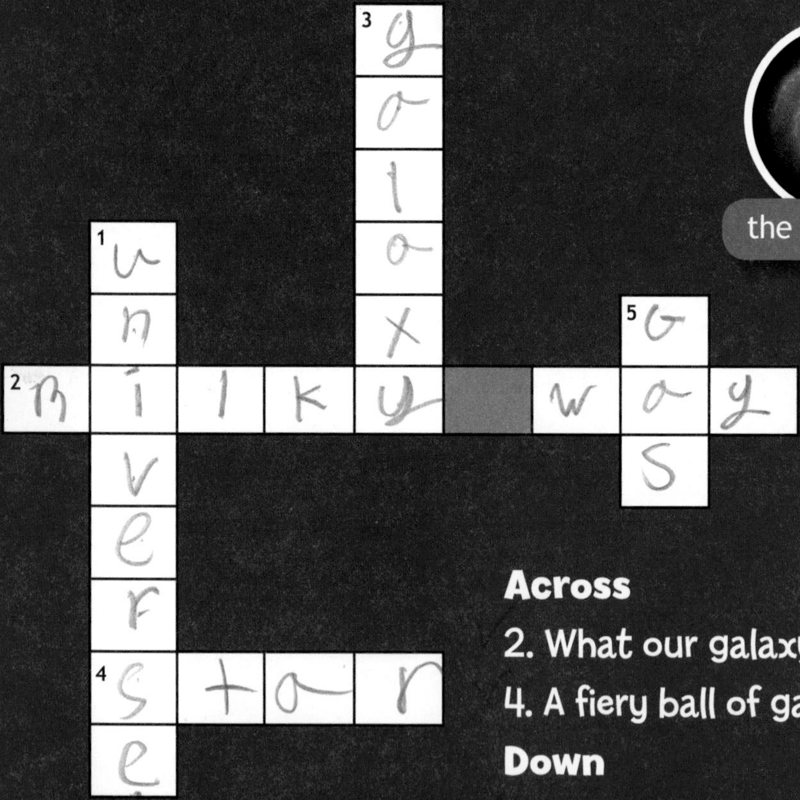

the Milky Way

Across

2. What our galaxy is called
4. A fiery ball of gas

Down

1. Everything in space
3. A huge group of stars
5. What the Sun burns

TRUE or FALSE?

Check the correct box to show which statements are true and which are false.

T F

☐ ☒ The Milky Way is bigger than the universe.

☑ ☐ Our solar system is part of the Milky Way.

☑ ☐ A star is a the size of a small ball.

☐ ☐ There are two galaxies in the universe.

☑ ☐ The Sun is a star.

☐ ☒ The Milky Way looks like spilled milk across the night sky.

TALK LIKE A SCIENTIST

Make up a poem or song about stars. Use your Smart Words. Share your poem or song with a friend.

CHAPTER 2

A Star Is Born

A star is born, lives, and then dies. That's the **life cycle** of a star. A new star is formed from a very cold cloud of dust and gas.

What do you think the cloud in this picture looks like?

Horsehead Nebula

SMART WORD

life cycle: changes over the life of an animal, plant, or object in space

A new star is formed when clumps of gas and dust come together in space. The clumps become tighter and hotter. When the clump gets hot enough, a new star is born!

the making of a star

dust and gas

new star

Leftover dust and gas surround most new stars. Some of this dust becomes planets in the star's new solar system!

Heat and Light

The middle of a star is the **core**, just like the core in an apple. A star's core is very important. That is where the star makes heat and light.

the core of a star

core

A star can burn for many years. But large stars burn faster than smaller stars.

Our Sun is a middle-sized star. It burns slowly so it will keep shining for 10 billion years! Some gigantic stars may burn up and die in a few million years.

Stars come in different sizes.

Sun

SMART WORD

core: the center part of a star where it makes heat and light

Colorful Stars

When scientists look at stars, they see different colors. Some are red, some are yellow, some are white, and some are blue. The smallest and coolest stars are red stars. The largest and hottest ones are blue. The Sun is a yellow star and middle-sized.

a blue star

blue star

Earth's Sun is a yellow star.

When a star uses up most of its gas, it begins to die. The star gets bigger. Huge stars like blue stars become red supergiants. Small and middle-sized stars become red giants. One day, our Sun will become a red giant!

red supergiant star

When a Star Dies

When a red giant star begins to die, huge clouds of dust and gas are blown away. The core of the star collapses and cools. This forms a white dwarf.

a red giant star at the end of its life

A red supergiant star explodes at the end of its life.

The explosion forms a **supernova**. It is very bright. The stardust from the explosion might form new planets or stars!

a red supergiant star before it exploded

a supernova exploding

SMART WORD

supernova: the very bright explosion of a red supergiant star

USE YOUR

SMART WORDS

Use these Smart Words to fill in each blank:

core   life cycle   supernova

The _____ of a star is
when it is born, lives, and then dies.

supernova

The middle of a star is its __core__.

The bright explosion of a red supergiant
star is called a __supernova__.

TALK LIKE A SCIENTIST

Draw a picture to show the life of a star. Tell a
friend or a member of your family about your
picture. Remember to use your Smart Words.

DRAW A STARRY NIGHT!

The artist who painted this picture wanted to show a wonderful starry night. Use paper and crayons or paint to create your own starry night picture.

Vincent Van Gogh, *Starry Night*

CHAPTER 3

Stargazing

Astronomers are people who study the stars, planets, and space. They use **telescopes** to look at stars. A telescope makes faraway things look closer and bigger. Some telescopes are on the Earth and some have been sent into space.

A telescope is used to study stars.

Stars are hard to see in a city because the lights are too bright. That is why most big telescopes on Earth are located far away from cities.

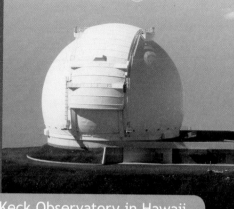

W.M. Keck Observatory in Hawaii

That is also why the Hubble Space Telescope was sent to travel around Earth and send back pictures. Space is a good place for a telescope because there are no bright lights up there!

Hubble Space Telescope

SMART WORDS

astronomer: a person who studies stars, planets, and space

telescope: an instrument used to make faraway objects in space look closer and bigger

Pictures in the Sky

Long ago, people did not know much about stars. They did not have telescopes to help them see things far away. They would look at the stars and see patterns or pictures in the sky. They would tell stories about the pictures. These groups of stars are called **constellations**.

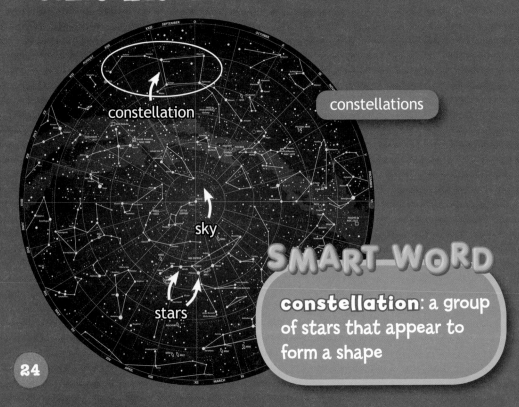

constellation

constellations

sky

stars

SMART WORD

constellation: a group of stars that appear to form a shape

The storytellers named the constellations after people, objects, or animals. Sometimes they were make-believe creatures like unicorns or dragons.

dragon constellation

Sometimes the constellations were named after real animals like bears or dogs.

Big Bear constellation

Telling Time

People long ago didn't have clocks. They had to use the Sun to know what time it was. During the day, the Sun seemed to go across the sky. The location of the Sun in the sky helped people know the time of day.

The setting Sun tells you it's time for bed!

the Sun at different times of the day

The stars told people about the seasons. People figured out that they saw some constellations only at certain times of the year.

Farmers looked at star patterns to find out when it was time to plant and when it was time to harvest. They used the stars to tell the time of year — just like a calendar!

planting time

harvesting time

Finding Our Way

Before maps or smartphones, people used the stars to help them **navigate**. The stars helped them to know where they were and where they wanted to go. The positions of the stars in the sky would help them to find directions.

A sextant helped people navigate by measuring the position of stars.

sextant

SMART WoRD

navigate: to find out where you are and where you need to go

The night sky looks different from different places on Earth. In the North, we see the North Star. So, we can use it to find where north is.

North Star

But people in the south, like Australia, cannot see the North Star. They use the Southern Cross to find their way.

Southern Cross constellation

Stars are important to us in so many ways!

USE YOUR SMART WORDS

Fill in each blank with a Smart Word.

> astronomer   constellation   navigate   telescope

A _____ is something that helps you to look at faraway stars.

Sailors used the stars to _____ at night.

A _____ is a group of stars that show a picture in the sky.

An _____ studies stars and planets.

TALK LIKE A SCIENTIST

Pretend you do not have a clock. How do you use the sky to tell you when to go to school or when to go to bed? Use your Smart Words.

SMART WORDS GLOSSARY

astronomer: a person who studies stars, planets, and space

constellation: a group of stars that appear to form a shape

core: the center part of a star where it makes heat and light

galaxy: a large group of stars

gas: a substance like air that does not have a hard surface

life cycle: changes over the life of an animal, plant, or object in space

Milky Way: our galaxy, which includes our solar system and many others

navigate: to find out where you are and where you need to go

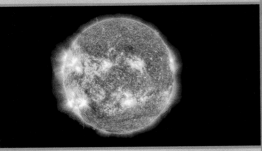

star: a huge ball of very hot and glowing gases

supernova: the very bright explosion of a red supergiant star

telescope: an instrument used to make faraway objects in space look closer and bigger

universe: all of space and everything in it, including all solar systems and galaxies

USE YOUR SMART WORDS ANSWERS

PAGE 10: ACROSS 2. Milky Way 4. star DOWN 1. universe 3. galaxy 5. gas

PAGE 11: F, T, F, F, T, T

PAGE 20: life cycle, core, supernova

PAGE 30: telescope, navigate, constellation, astronomer